Pub Walks Near Hungerford

by Alex Milne-White

Published by Milne-White Books Ltd.

First edition

Published by Milne-White Books Ltd.

ISBN 978-0-9570027-0-8

Copyright © 2011 Milne-White Books Ltd.

Photography (cover and internal) by Alex Milne-White
www.hungerfordbooks.co.uk

Design, typesetting and illustrations by Adrian Robinson
www.writecreative.net

Printed by Mayfield Press, Oxford

Pub Walks Near Hungerford

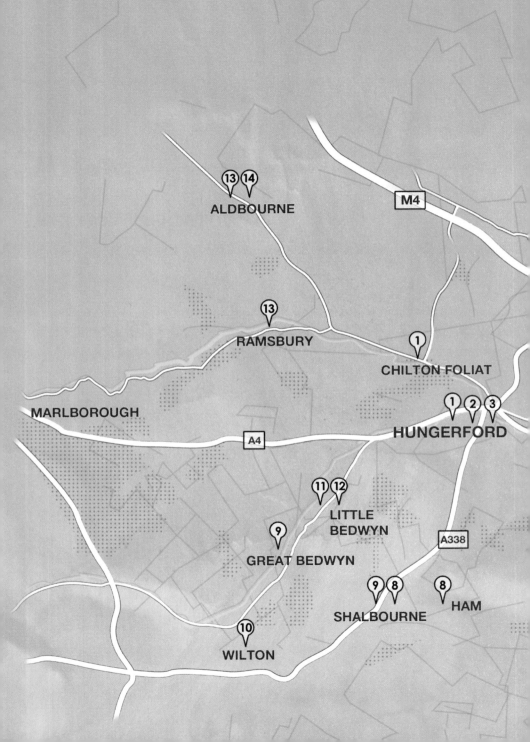

Index of walks

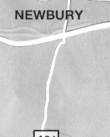

M4

4

WICKHAM

3

KINTBURY

A4

NEWBURY

7 6 INKPEN

A34

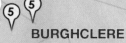

SANDHAM   5   5

BURGHCLERE

Acknowledgements

I'd like to thank the West Berkshire Ramblers for producing the book upon which some of these walks are based and for allowing me to update and reproduce those walks.

Mainly I'd like to thank Emma for minding the shop, in various stages of pregnancy, while I gallivanted around the local countryside talking into a Dictaphone. The last walk was completed only a week before little Hattie arrived and oddly enough it's been a bit difficult to get out for much of a walk since then! Perhaps, the next book should be on child-friendly walks in the area.

Introduction

I'm not really a rambler, so I'm not going to start telling you what equipment you should take with you on a walk. I know sturdy walking shoes are generally a good idea, but as long as you are not going to be clambering up rocky slopes (unlikely around here) I usually find a good pair of trainers adequate – although woody walks can get quite muddy, and porous shoes can be a mistake in very muddy conditions! As for coats etc I'm sure you're sensible enough to check the forecast beforehand and dress/pack accordingly.

I have always loved walking and I'm a keen photographer as well, so when my wife (Emma) and I moved to Hungerford to buy the bookshop, we soon realised what a great area for walking this is. When the previous book of local walks '21 Walks for the 21st Century' went out of print there was a definite gap in the market that needed filling. Some of the walks in this book are taken from that book, although they've all been walked (in 2010) and updated where necessary, some are similar, and others are completely new walks (to me anyway).

The walks in this book are all circular (I never like going back on myself) and all feature at least one pub, usually at the start, and often have an option for another one part way round. This might make me sound like an alcoholic, but I've found the best way to entice Emma out for a strenuous walk is the inducement of a drink and/or meal half way round. As many of the walks start at a pub parking at the pub would seem logical, but bear in mind that they are for patrons only so you'll either have to visit the pub at some point or find an alternative parking spot.

If I'm not a rambler then I'm definitely not a birdwatcher, but over the course of researching these walks, and driving around this area, I've seen a lot of Red Kites (or the same few, many times) and I've developed a deep affection for these graceful creatures. In particular there seem to be three that go around together in the area just south of the M4 near the Hungerford junction, so keep an eye out for these as you walk.

Abbreviations and other notes

The only Abbreviation I've used is FP for footpath.

The walk distances are approximated to the nearest half mile. The times are of course approximate, as everyone walks at different speeds, but they are based on how long it took me as I'm a pretty quick walker (even with stopping for photos and recording directions).

The maps with each walk are accurate and pretty much to scale, but it's always a good idea to take the relevant OS map as they are detailed and will help more if you stray from the directions!

All walks are covered by **Ordnance survey maps Explorer 157 & 158**.

Walk 1

Hungerford to Chilton Foliat

Chilton Foliat is a lovely little village, with lots of thatched cottages, which runs alongside the River Kennet. This is a varied and quite easy walk, with just a couple of minor climbs. The Wheatsheaf is an old fashioned kind of pub, and is currently up for sale, so I can't guarantee it will remain a pub, but fingers crossed that it does.

Hopgrass Farm has been a successful farm for nearly 500 years. In the 1980/90s television presenter Johnny Morris and his wife lived in Hopgrass Barn and they are both buried nearby. Whether or not he erected the statue of Morecambe and Wise in the grounds I can't seem to find out!

Distance: 6 miles

Time: 2½ hours

OS map: Explorer 158

Time to **The Wheatsheaf pub**: 1½ hours

1. Start in **Hungerford**, possibly at the station car park (SU340685), and make your way down to the **Kennet and Avon Canal** and proceed left on the towpath.

2. Walk past lock, then **St Lawrence's Church**, past the swing bridge in **Freeman's Marsh** and one more lock until you reach stepped bridge over the canal.

3. Cross the bridge and follow footpath sign across field to reach the **A4***. Turn left for 100 metres then cross the road at entrance to **Highclose**, and continue for another 100 metres on the **A4** to signed footpath on right. *You can turn right here to Cobbs farm shop for some breakfast or lunch.*

4. Take footpath up through gap in trees, over or around log barrier, and turn right at footpath arrow. Keep **Cake Wood** on your left, then at end of wood proceed ahead and slightly to the left across field to dip in trees.

5. Take path between woods and follow round to the right, keeping **Brickkiln Copse** on your right. Continue on path into field and then left after farm building and down to the road.

6. Go round gate onto road and turn left briefly, then right following footpath marked (faintly) to **Chilton Foliat**. Follow path through lovely woods, over footbridge across **The Kennet**, along to another small bridge, and out into **Chilton Foliat**.

7. Turn right and walk through village, past **The Wheatsheaf pub**, and follow road round to the right, over **The Kennet**. When road bends sharp left, cross it and follow path signed **Hungerford** up hill.

8. At top of hill bear right, following footpath sign, up a short steep climb through the woods and then out into a field. Follow path across field to reach a track. Turn right on track and follow round to the right, then left, down to the road.

9. Turn left on **A4**, then turn right following footpath sign past Hopgrass. Go through gate into **Freeman's Marsh** and cross the footbridge, then turn immediately left and follow path alongside the river.

10. Go through gate and across small bridge along to another gate. Follow path, ignoring gate on your left, to reach another gate, bridge, and gate, then cross swing bridge and take the path straight on through the grounds of **St. Lawrence's Church**.

11. Turn left and walk through **The Croft**, down an alleyway and onto the **High Street**. For **Station** car park turn right, under railway bridge, then immediately left up **The Cuttings** back to the station.

Walk 1
Hungerford to Chilton Foliat

CHILTON FOLIAT

The Kennet

Littlecote Home Farm

LEVERTON

Hopgrass Farm

Cake Wood

...hclose House

HUNGERFORD

5

Walk 2

Hungerford to Little Hidden Farm

Little Hidden Farm is a mixed organic farm that also has educational tours in the summer and runs a riding school. It's just up the road from Hungerford Newtown where the Tally Ho pub provides a good stopping point for the hungry or thirsty walker. This is a good walk for nature lovers as I've seen hares in the fields after Great Hidden Farm and twice spotted three Red Kites circling near Little Hidden Farm.

Distance: 6 miles

Time: 2½ hours

OS map: Explorer 158

Time to **The Tally Ho pub**: Just over 1 hour

1. Start in **Hungerford**, at the station car park (SU340685), and make your way down to the **Kennet & Avon Canal**, cross the small bridge and follow the footpath to emerge onto **Bridge Street** next to the **John O'Gaunt pub**. Turn right to the mini-roundabout and turn right again.

2. Walk past the 1st petrol station and cross the road. Cross over **The Kennet** and take the first left on the road (ignoring the footpath). Follow the road round to the **A338**, cross over carefully and turn left up the hill, past **St Saviour's Cemetery** until you reach a footpath sign on your right.

3. Cross stile and go straight on through field. There is a footpath through wood on left, but it's easier to walk around edge of wood and turn left through gate. Head half right across field towards a stile on the right edge just before the taller trees.

4. Cross stile into next field and bear left skirting around the crops, then head half right to stile, which is about half way along the row of trees. Cross stile onto lane and go right for 250 metres to a footpath sign on left.

5. Follow footpath over stile and then along the right edge of field. When you reach a track go left towards **Great Hidden Farm**. Cross cattle grid and bear half right to stile in corner of field, cross this and proceed along right edge of fields.

6. Keep crossing stiles in the same direction until you reach a gate. After gate turn left following footpath sign to walk on right side of fence. Cross stile and carry straight on down almost to the road*. Turn left on footpath along right edge of field until you emerge opposite the entrance to **Little Hidden Farm**. *You can turn right at this point down to **The Tally Ho pub**.

7. Cross the **A338** with care, and follow footpath sign up tarmac track. At crossroad of footpaths carry straight on, then turn right at next footpath sign, through three gates and turn left behind farm. *Watch out for Red Kites here.

8. Kink slightly left to carry on along right edge of field. Follow path around right edge of next field as it skirts a hollow then, ignoring gates in corner, turn left, still in the same field, until you reach a gate at far right corner. Go through gate and proceed straight across field and out onto lane.

9. Turn left on lane then turn right following bridlepath sign (ignore footpath sign). Skirt left edge of farm initially, then when the tarmac track forks take the right fork and follow all the way to a minor road and turn left.

More instructions overleaf »

Walk 2
Hungerford to Little Hidden Farm

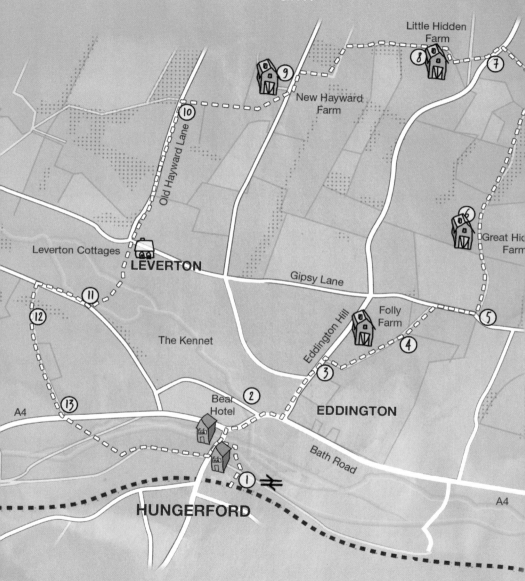

Little Hidden Farm

8

7

9

New Hayward Farm

10

Old Hayward Lane

6

Great Hi Far

Leverton Cottages

LEVERTON

Gipsy Lane

5

The Kennet

11

12

Eddington Hill

Folly Farm

4

3

13

A4

Bear Hotel

2

EDDINGTON

Bath Road

1

HUNGERFORD

A4

10. Follow road all the way down to **Leverton** and at crossing go straight on, past **The Leverton Cottages,** on footpath. Carry on across river and round to the left, then turn right, and shortly right again, then across two footbridges and up steps to road.

11. Turn right on road, crossing into Wiltshire, for about 300 metres, until you see a footpath sign on left marked **Hungerford 1½**. Cross road carefully and follow this path straight up to top of the hill. *Look behind you for a great view of* ***Chilton Lodge***.

12. Go through trees and follow sign along left edge of field, then follow arrow to go along right edge of neighbouring field. At end of fields cross stile and go down steps to the **A4**. Cross with care to footpath sign on your left.

13. Follow path through gap, then half left across field. Go through gate and turn left towards **St Lawrence's church**, cross gate, bridge, and another gate, then cross swing bridge and turn left along towpath back into **Hungerford**. If parked at station continue on the towpath until you see the first bridge you crossed and turn right up to the station.

Walk 3

Hungerford to Kintbury

This is a pleasant, flat walk, which is quite varied. It passes right by The Blue Ball in Kintbury or you can easily divert to The Dundas Arms, which has a lovely setting by the canal and does very good food (although oddly not at Sunday lunchtime). Starting at the Downgate pub (at the end of Park Street in Hungerford) is probably simplest, but you can shorten the walk a little by parking in the middle of the common or in the small carpark near Dunn Mill, or to really shorten it you follow the walk up to Step 10 and get the train back. St Cassian's Centre is a residential retreat centre, run by a mixed community of Brothers, lay staff, gap-year volunteers and support staff. It was founded in 1975 to provide retreat experiences for young people.

Distance: 7 miles

Time: 2½–3 hours

OS map: Explorer 158

Time to **Blue Ball pub**: Just over 1 hour

Time to **Dundas Arms**: 1½–1¾ hour

1. Start from **The Downgate pub** car park (SU342383) and walk across common heading just right of tall trees, then follow footpath sign at side of road to stile at far corner of common. (or you can park by the track leading from the junction in the middle of the common).

2. Cross stile and follow clear path along field edge until you reach a minor road.

3. Proceed left, briefly along road, then right at footpath sign along fenced path to stile.

4. Follow left edge of field, cross next stile and follow direction of footpath sign across field. Cross track and next field, then follow footpath sign into next field straight on past marked crossroad of footpaths with **St Cassian's** on your right.

5. Cross road leading to **St Cassian's** and follow footpath sign into copse. Follow path as it opens out into wide track to stile.

6. Cross field and next stile then veer left to pass broken stile. Follow right edge of next field and over two stiles.

7. Bear right, crossing stream, then left crossing field diagonally to cross a wobbly stile to a road.

8. Go left on road then at junction bear left (ignoring footpath signs). When the road veers left at entrance to **Titcomb Manor** cross stile on right.

9. Follow left edge of field to reach next stile, then keep right in next field until you reach gate. Go through and follow clear path all the way into **Kintbury**. *Blue Bell pub* now on right.

10. Cross road following footpath sign onto track. Bear left past pub beer garden, then go through gate into churchyard and take left hand path down to and crossing canal bridge. *Dundas Arms pub* and *train station* now 100 metres on right.

11. Turn left onto canal towpath and follow until you have to cross bridge before third lock.

12. Turn right onto towpath then follow path into field left of towpath. Carry on until you see a tunnel under the railway.

13. Go through tunnel then turn right, up the hill, and follow in the direction of the church spire until you can see your starting point.

Walk 3
Hungerford to Kintbury

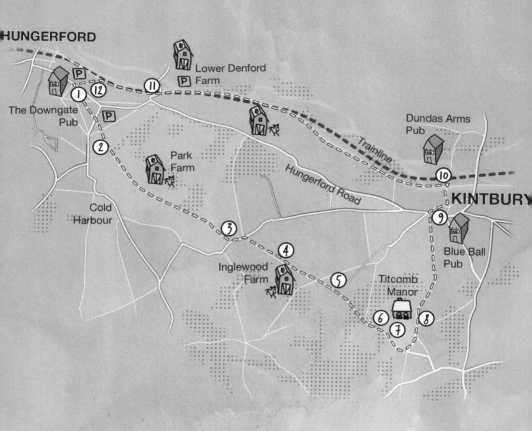

HUNGERFORD

The Downgate Pub

Lower Denford Farm

Cold Harbour

Park Farm

Inglewood Farm

Hungerford Road

Trainline

Dundas Arms Pub

KINTBURY

Blue Ball Pub

Titcomb Manor

Walk 4

Around Wickham

This is a pleasant and varied walk from the small town of Wickham, and it is mostly flat. Again on this walk I saw three Red Kites circling and I'm pretty sure they're the same ones as I've seen near Little Hidden Farm. I did have a slight incident with some aggressive cows on this walk, but I'm sure by the time you read this they will have gone or moved to a different field – they say that adopting a confident/aggressive stance will put aggressive cows off, but I made a run for it, just to be on the safe side!

Distance: 5 miles

Time: 2 hours

OS map: Explorer 158

1. Park on the strip at the front of **The Five Bells pub** (SU395718) and walk to the right edge of the pub's grounds where a small footpath leads between two fences. When you emerge onto playing field turn right.

2. Head for, and through, gap at right corner of field and onto track. Follow track down to road, cross road and take track opposite. Turn immediately right through kissing gate and bear diagonally left across field keeping right of large lone tree, then row of trees, to reach a gate near the far right corner of field.

3. Go through gate and follow path into woods until you reach a T-junction of footpaths, turn left. As you join a wider path turn left and follow until you emerge from the woods and pass two small houses. Follow track to its end and turn left.

4. Stay on track as it bears right, and turn sharp right in front of large barn. Follow right edge of small field, then the left edge of the much larger field. Cross small road and follow footpath sign into field, heading diagonally left to corner of track.

5. Join path and carry straight on to the junction of paths and turn right on path through middle of field. Follow path as it passes **Sole Farm**, then go straight on into woods. Follow main path through woods until you come to a footpath sign pointing right.

6. Follow this small path past a pond on your left and through the bracken filled woods, past a timber yard on your right, across a track, until directed left by a yellow arrow. Follow this wider track to road, cross road and follow footpath sign opposite across stile into field.

7. Take path at left edge of field and follow as it bears right, then look out for unmarked stile on left. Cross stile and head directly across field to stile at far side*. Continue in same direction across next field to gap in trees, then bear half left across field towards next gap in trees. *Watch out for aggressive cows.

8. At crossing of a byway continue straight on across next field, through another gap in trees and straight on again, this time along right edge of next field. At end of field take small road opposite, signposted **Clapton**.

9. Ignore footpath on left, but when the road bears left go straight on on public bridleway. Follow bridleway until its end and turn right on restricted byway. At end of byway carry straight on onto track, ignoring footpath on right, and follow to the main road. Turn right back to your starting point.

Walk 4
Around Wickham

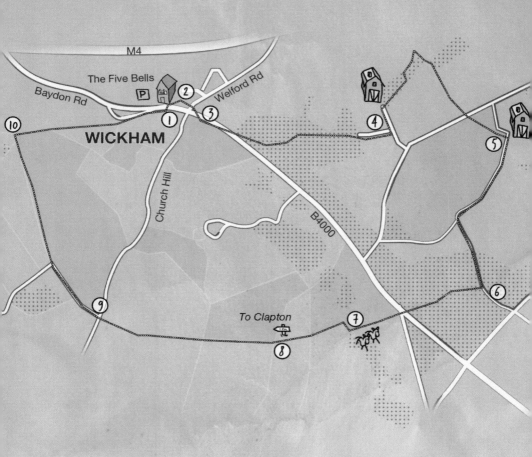

M4

The Five Bells

Baydon Rd

Welford Rd

WICKHAM

Church Hill

B4000

To Clapton

Walk 5

Burghclere and Sandham Memorial Chapel

This walk is a bit further afield than most, but it's worth it for a lovely walk with open fields, woodland and a section of disused railway line, plus you can pay a visit to the impressive Sandham Memorial Chapel. Burghclere is a few miles south on Newbury, just off the A34.

Sandham Memorial Chapel was completed in 1932, and was built to house the paintings of Stanley Spencer. The paintings cover the entire wall space of the small chapel and illustrate the artist's experiences as a medical orderly in a war hospital in Bristol and the northern Greek region of Macedonia during the First World War. It's open weekends from March to December, plus Wed-Fri April to October, but it's worth checking opening times before you visit.

Distance: 4 miles

Time: 1½ hours

OS map: Explorer 158

1. Park in lay-by opposite **Sandham Memorial Chapel** (SU463608), or at **The Carpenter's Arms** if you're planning to visit the pub, and walk west, past the pub on the road, until you reach a cul-de-sac on the left, take this road.

2. Near end of lane, take footpath on the right. Cross stile into field and cross field in same direction until you reach a gap in the far left corner (there are two stiles, but the gap negates them). Go through gap and left across next field.

3. Cross stile at end of field and turn right on footpath between trees. Cross stile into field and follow path initially left, then branch right towards a gap in the trees at the far end of field. Go through gap and turn left, ignoring more obvious path straight on, and follow left edge of field, then turn left across wooden boards and up slope to reach disused railway line.

4. Turn right on path and walk for a few hundred metres until you see paths going off on both sides, take the left path down and through gate into field. Follow left edge of field and go through gate onto road.

5. Take small road opposite, signposted **Dodd's Farm**, then dogleg slightly left through farm and onto track. Follow right edge of field to stile at far right corner (you may have to duck under or over a couple of wire fences to get there, as the farmer seems to be ignoring the right of way!)

6. Cross stile and keep to right edge of next field to reach broken stile at right corner. Cross this stile and bear diagonally right across field. Turn left at end of path and bear just left of **Pheasant Cottage** to reach track.

7. Turn left on track and follow the main path for about a mile until its end. Take the road opposite, signposted **Sandham Memorial Chapel**, and follow to the end, then cross the main road and take the footpath opposite, next to a driveway.

8. At end of path go through metal gate and continue in same direction along left edge of field. Go through next metal gate and turn left on **Ox Drove**. Continue as track turns into road, then turn left at end of road. At the end of this road turn right and back to your starting point.

Walk 5
Burghclere and Sandham Memorial Chapel

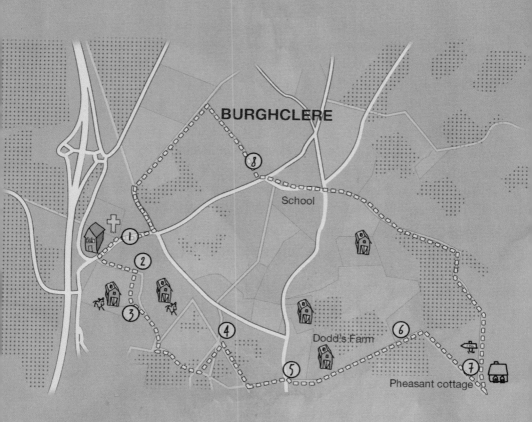

BURGHCLERE

School

Dodd's Farm

Pheasant cottage

Walk 6

Inkpen and the Coombe Gibbet

The Coombe Gibbet was erected in 1676 for the purpose of gibbeting the bodies of George Broomham and Dorothy Newman, who were having an affair and were hanged for murdering George's wife and son after they discovered them together on the downs. The gibbet was placed in such a prominent location as a warning, to deter others from committing crimes. It has only ever been used for them. The current gibbet is a replica of the original, which was destroyed many years ago.

This is a great, varied walk, with the effort of a fairly steep climb early on rewarded by great views from the downs - Walbury Hill being the highest point in South East England. Parking is limited in Inkpen so I've suggested parking at the Crown and Anchor, but if you are doing so you should have a meal or a drink there either before or after, it's a nice pub with good food. The walk also passes close by to Inkpen's other pub, The Swan, if you want sustenance on the way. If you don't know where the Crown and Anchor is check a map first, because it's very easy to get lost in Inkpen!

Distance: 6 miles

Time: 2¼ hours

OS map: Explorer 158

Time to **The Swan pub:** 1¾ hours

Time to **Crown and Anchor:** 2¼ hours

1. Start from **Crown and Anchor pub** car park (SU378639) and walk down the Byway that leads out of the rear of the pub.

2. At crossroads of footpaths carry straight on, then along lane for about five minutes. At road junction turn right and follow road until it bears right.

3. Follow second footpath sign along right edge of field all the way to the corner, then follow small sign into copse. When path reaches road cross and take path between two roads up hill to a stile.

4. Cross stile and head across field, keeping the large trough on your left, to another (unnecessary!) stile. Pass this stile and follow line of path up to a stile. Cross onto wide path and turn right to cross **Walbury Hill**.

5. Follow path to road, cross onto **The Test Way** and along to cross stile up to the **Coombe Gibbet**.

6. Cross next stile back onto wide path and continue until the path turns left, then right, then go through gate on the right.

7. Walk to and cross stile on left, then follow track down hill as it bends around to the left. At bottom of hill follow arrow back right, then left down to gate.

8. Follow path, keeping straight on at junction, then round to left and through two gates to reach road.

9. Turn right on road, then right at junction along to footpath sign on left. Follow this path along left edge of field, across two stiles, and onto road.

10. Turn right and at junction take footpath opposite, up between houses, around a field, across footbridge and two kissing gates then round to the right as it passes **Manor Farm**.

11. Cross road to take footpath opposite, across field, through kissing gates and onto lane.

12. Turn right and follow road, past recreation ground on your left to main road. Cross and take the footpath opposite, through kissing gate across field and through second gate onto track.

13. Turn left and follow main path through woods, turning right at junction of footpaths to reach road and starting point.

Walk 6
Inkpen and the Coombe Gibbet

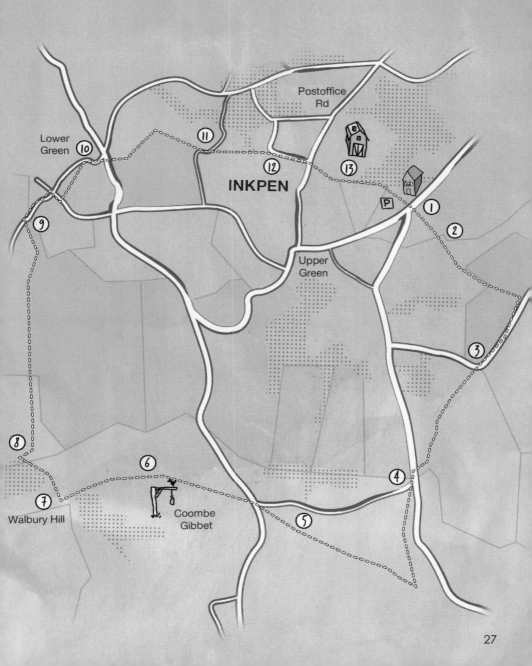

Postoffice Rd

Lower Green ⑩

⑪

⑫

INKPEN

⑬

P

①

②

Upper Green

③

Walbury Hill ⑦

⑧

⑥

Coombe Gibbet

⑤

④

⑨

Walk 7

Inkpen

A pleasant, easy-going walk around the west side of Inkpen. The Swan is an old fashioned sort of pub, with a restaurant attached , plus its own organic farm shop.

Distance: 5 miles
Time: 1¾ hours
OS map: Explorer 158

1. Park at, or near, **The Swan pub** (SU359643) in **Inkpen**. Walk west along the main road, for about 100 metres, until you see a footpath sign on your left and follow through gate into small field and across to gate at far side. Go through gate and turn left on Byway.

2. Walk to end of path and turn right on restricted byway. Ignore byways first on the left, then the right side, and continue as path narrows, until you eventually see a footpath sign on right.

3. Follow this path until you reach a gate in the left corner of field. Go through gate and cross field just right of straight on towards a footpath sign. Turn right at sign to reach gate, go through gate into field and cross again just right of straight on to a stile at the far side.

4. Cross stile and take path through woods until you emerge on track next to gate. Go through gate and cross field straight across to another gate, go through and bear half right to stile next to gate. Cross stile and cross field to reach gate at far left corner.

5. Go through gate and follow left edge of field around to a kissing gate. Go through gate and cross next field to another kissing gate, go through this and pass some stables to reach another gate.

6. Go through gate and turn half right onto gravel track. When track joins concrete road turn left and follow to lane and turn left. At end of lane bear left and cross main road to public bridleway sign opposite.

7. Follow bridleway into and through woods until you reach a large gate. Go through and continue on path between fields until you reach a five-way junction of paths, take the rightmost path.

8. Follow path past redundant stile into trees, over footbridge and right up to stile. Cross stile and follow right edge of field, across stile and along right edge of next field to another stile. Cross and turn right on lane. Cross stile next to gate and turn right on road.

9. At footpath sign on right cross stile into field and follow the right edge. At end turn right across footbridge and along path by stream until you reach a gate. After gate, turn left and follow path to main road. Turn right and follow road back to **The Swan**.

Walk 7

Inkpen

Walk 8
Ham and Shalbourne

Ham and Shalbourne are both lovely villages on the border of Wiltshire and Berkshire. This fairly short and pleasant walk forms a rough circle between the two. You will pass The Plough in Shalbourne is about three quarters of the way round and it's a good pub with nice food, alternatively The Crown and Anchor in Ham is a nice little pub, which serves very nice Indian food in the restaurant section. Also the post office & store in Shalbourne has a little coffee shop inside, with tables on the pavement in good weather.

Distance: 5 miles
Time: 2 hours
OS map: Explorer 158
Time to **The Plough pub**: 1½ hours

1. Park at, or near, the **Crown & Anchor pub** in **Ham** (SU331631). Head up the road, going left at the junction, to a footpath sign on right. Cross stile.

2. Cross field to stile, cross and go round pond. Head for and cross stile at left corner of gardens. Bear left across field to next stile, cross and turn left through gap in trees into large field.

3. The way is not clear at this stage. Follow the track into centre of field, then when track bears left, head diagonally right up towards two large trees. As you approach you should see a footpath sign.

4. Cross road and go along avenue towards **Mount Prosperous**. Follow the track left, right, then left again, then at footpath sign carry straight on towards gate in left corner of field.

5. Cross stile and proceed down (muddy) woodland path. Continue on hedge path, through a squeeze stile and along to the **A338**.

6. Cross with care, then follow footpath sign on the right across a field to a stile. Cross next field and stile onto road and turn right.

7. Follow road up, over river, until you reach some farm buildings on the left. Turn left and you should now see a footpath sign on your left. Take path into field.

8. Walk along right edge of field and when field opens out at footpath sign carry straight on to reach a stile. Cross stiles on either side of road then follow path along the banks of the river until you reach the road.

9. Turn left over bridge, then cross **A338** with care, and follow footpath sign opposite into field. Keep trees on your right to cross a footbridge at the right corner of field.

10. Go straight on, past footpaths to either side, then across stile, road and another stile onto fenced path.

11. Follow path round to right, then across two more stiles and fields to a kissing gate. You can skip to *Step 16* here if you don't want to go into **Shalbourne**.

12. Turn right down **Cox's Lane** to the road through Shalbourne and turn left to reach **The Plough pub**. Take road opposite the pub and follow footpath sign on left, up houses' drives, to a fence path. Go through gate and across field to stile onto **Cox's Lane** again.

13. Go through gate next to the one you came through in *Step 13* and follow this fenced path until it opens out into field. Head diagonally to far corner of field.

14. Go left on track, then follow round to the left, then right, until you see a small gate on your right into a field. Go through gate and bear left to reach gate at far end of field. Cross onto road and turn left to come out opposite the **Crown & Anchor pub**.

Walk 8
Ham and Shalbourne

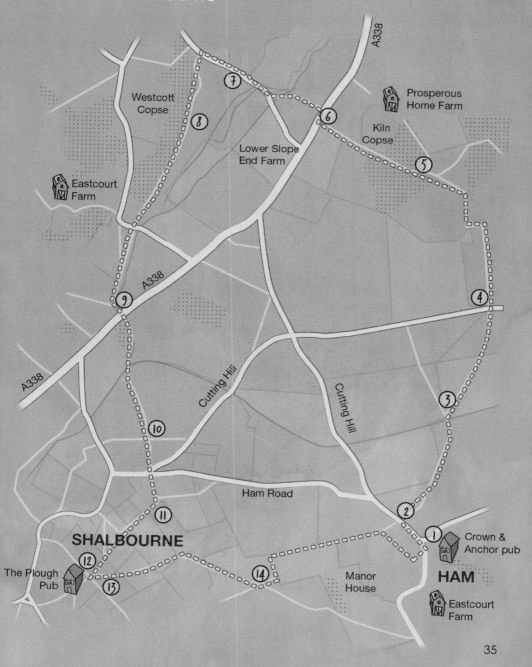

A338

⑦

Westcott Copse

⑧

Eastcourt Farm

Lower Slope End Farm

A338

⑥

Kiln Copse

Prosperous Home Farm

⑤

⑨

A338

A338

④

Cutting Hill

Cutting Hill

③

⑩

Ham Road

②

⑪

SHALBOURNE

① Crown & Anchor pub

⑫

The Plough Pub

⑬

⑭

Manor House

HAM

Eastcourt Farm

Walk 9

Great Bedwyn to Shalbourne

Great Bedwyn is another lovely village, with two good pubs and its own railway station, as well as the Kennet and Avon running through. It's a nice, varied walk, which is fairly hilly, but nothing too strenuous. You'll pass The Plough pub in Shalbourne about half way through, which is a good pub with decent food, or you can visit either of Great Bedwyns' pubs at the end.

One of the largest Roman villas in Britain was discovered in 1780 near to the line of the Roman road from Winchester to Cirencester, it was excavated in the 1990s, but is now fully re-buried.

Distance: 6 miles

Time: 2½ hours

OS map: Explorer 158

Time to **The Plough pub**: 1¼ hours

1. Park at, or near, **Great Bedwyn Station** (SU280645), or at the car park after the canal bridge. If parked in **Great Bedwyn** start by walking over the railway and canal bridges.

2. Take the road on the left, signposted to **Village Hall**. Continue to bridlepath sign on right signed **Jockey Green**. Follow the bridlepath until you join the road, then take gravel path on left next to various footpath signs (currently pointing in wrong directions!).

3. Follow path around to the right and then all the way until you come to a concrete road, turn left for 200 metres. Take tarmac footpath on right through centre of field. After new plantation on right fork right across field to small footbridge.

4. Cross footbridge and walk up gravel track for a few metres before veering left through field into gap in woods. There are no footpaths signs, but follow the clear path through the woods, over track, and out into field. Continue in a straight line across the field towards a blue drum at edge of field. Pass this and follow yellow footpaths arrow to the right.

5. After about 20 metres follow yellow footpaths arrow to the left into corner of field, then follow left edge of field. After next footpaths sign go through gap into next field and go uphill on right edge of field. At top pass into adjacent field and follow left edge down to the bottom of the hill.

6. Pass through narrow gap to road. Cross the busy **A338** carefully, then follow footpath opposite straight through field (this can be quite hard work depending on how high the crops are!).

7. At bottom turn right along footpath at bottom of field. Turn left at footpath sign along wide path leading into Shalbourne. Turn right on main road through **Shalbourne** until you reach the post office, then **The Plough pub**.

8. Carry on on the road past **The Plough** for about 100 metres, then turn right following a footpath sign along the right edge of field. Cross over footbridge at end of field the bear right briefly and cross the stile on your left, and the next one to head up the hill.

9. At the top of the hill go straight on through gap in hedgerow to reach the **A338**. Cross carefully and follow footpath sign opposite, bearing slightly left across field. At brow of hill bear slightly right, next to straw bales, then continue straight on towards footpath signpost at far edge of field.

More instructions overleaf »

Walk 9
Great Bedwyn to Shalbourne

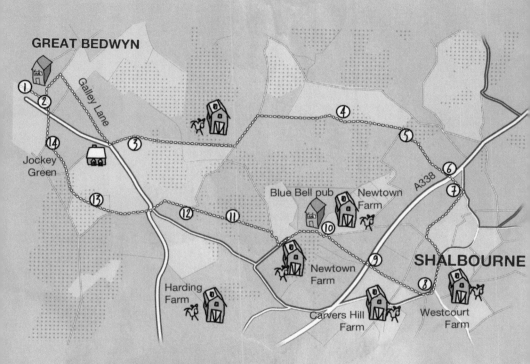

10. Go left on concrete track, then bear left following by-way sign, keeping house and farm on your right, then bear left onto lane. Turn right following bridlepath sign, then follow next sign diagonally left across field to enter copse following blue footpath arrow.

11. Follow clear path, over track, through woods and out into field. Head for gate at far right corner. Go through gate and turn left, keeping tennis court on your right, then right along to, and through, large gate on the right.

12. Turn left onto concrete bridlepath and follow this down to road. Cross road and walk up other road a few metres to reach footpath on right. Follow this tree-lined path until it opens out into field. Keep to left edge and then fork a little to the right to enter **Bedwyn Brail** to the left of the first blue drum.

13. Take the path through the woods as it becomes a wider track until it opens out into ferny area and turn right. Follow this path until it opens onto large field. Skirt around right edge of field to the far right corner.

14. Veer right on path through trees and into field, keep to left edge of field and follow path out of bottom left corner and down onto road. Turn left to reach your starting point.

Walk 10
Wilton and Crofton Beam Engines

This is a shorter walk than most, but it is pleasant and varied with plenty to see, including the steam pumping station at Crofton and the lovely village of Wilton, with an option to divert to Wilton Windmill. The Swan in Wilton is a lovely pub with great food. Wilton is about 5 miles south-west of Hungerford, just off the A338.

Wilton Windmill was built in 1821, when the creation of The Kennet and Avon canal made the water mills that previously operated on the River Bedwyn redundant, and was originally in operation for about 100 years before falling into disuse. It was restored by the Wiltshire Historic Buildings Trust in 1976 and is now the only working windmill in Wessex.

Distance: 3 miles
Time: 1¼ hours
OS map: Explorer 157

1. Park near **The Swan pub** (268615) in **Wilton** (or in its car park if you're going to go there). Walk past the pub along the road until you reach the pond. Take footpath opposite pond past the hedge then turn left.

2. Follow path alongside **Wilton Water** until you come to the **Kennet and Avon canal** opposite **Crofton Beam Engines***. Turn right on the canal towpath. *You can cross the canal and visit the pumping station here.*

3. Walk along towpath past two locks, then at a modern bridge, just after second lock turn right, on unmarked footpath, to walk up the right edge of field until you reach a stile at the wood's edge.

4. Cross stile into **Wilton Brail** and turn right. Keep on this path until you emerge from the woods. Continue in same direction across field, through gap in trees, across next field. Cross stile on to path down to track.

5. Turn left on track and follow down to road*. Turn right on road and follow into **Wilton** and back to your starting point. *You can turn left on road, then right for a few hundred metres here to visit Wilton Windmill.*

Walk 10
Wilton and Crofton Beam Engines

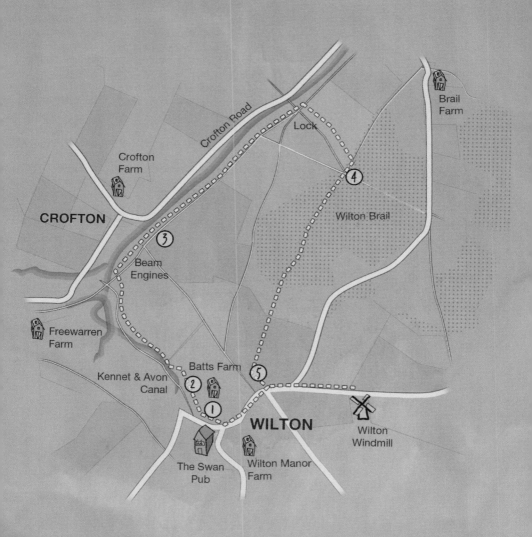

Brail
Farm

Crofton Road

Lock

Crofton
Farm

CROFTON

④

Wilton Brail

③

Beam
Engines

Freewarren
Farm

Batts Farm

Kennet & Avon
Canal

②

⑤

①

WILTON

Wilton
Windmill

The Swan
Pub

Wilton Manor
Farm

Walk 11

Little Bedwyn, Stype and Standen Manor

This is a lovely, mainly flat walk, with paths through woods, fields and by the canal, with a possible pub stop, via a short diversion, three quarters of the way around. Little Bedwyn is about three miles west of Hungerford, there is a signed turn-off from the A4 just before Froxfield.

Standen Manor is a very attractive, Grade II listed, country mansion. It was requisitioned by US troops during the Second World War during the 10-11 months prior to D-Day and they were visited there by General Eisenhower.

Distance: 6½ miles

Time: 2¼ hours

OS map: Explorer 158

Time to **The Pelican pub**: 1¾ hours

1. Park in **Little Bedwyn** next to the church (SU291662) and walk back along the road to the T-junction. Turn left and take the footbridge over the railway and canal, then turn right and then right, under the footbridge, along The **Kennet and Avon Canal** towpath.

2. After you pass a cottage on your right walk up the verge, before the bridge, and cross the road to take bridlepath opposite, signed **Jugg's Cottage**. Follow this path uphill, then down and around to the left, then when a bridlepath crosses, carry straight-on on smaller bridlepath.

3. At end of path turn left on track for about ten metres until you see a footpath sign pointing right. If you can't follow this path walk a little further and pass a large gate to follow the main path up the long straight track through the woods.

4. At the end, go through a metal kissing gate and go along track until it bears right with a white footpath sign on the right. Bear slightly right here to reach a large metal gate, go through and follow the white posts across this large field, with **Stype Grange** on your right, to reach another metal kissing gate.

5. Pass through gate and turn left on road for about 100 metres, looking out for an unmarked gate on the left. Go through this gate into field and bear half right, heading between two large trees, and then along edge of woods until you come across the remains of a stile on the left (with a pipe across a ditch after it).

6. Pass stile into woods and bear right on path that winds through the woods. When you emerge onto a larger path turn left and follow until the path broadens into a lane, just before **Standen Manor**. Follow public footpath sign to the left.

7. Go straight across field, bearing slightly right around end of copse, then along line of telegraph poles and into gap in woods. Follow path as it becomes fenced on both sides and carry straight on until the path ends at a road.

8. Turn left, ignoring two paths on the right, and walk along road for about 300 metres until you see a bridlepath sign on right. Go right, past the gate, and follow this path down to the road. At road junction turn right and walk along road until you see a gate on the left. To reach **The Pelican pub**, just carry on, on the road, for another 50 metres to the main road and you will see it on your left.

9. Go through the gate and down to the towpath and go left past three locks (and one bridge), then cross the canal at the next bridge, following footpath sign for **Froxfield Road**.

10. Cross railway line (with care), then turn immediately keeping the railway to your left. Cross a stile into an orchard, then continue past church and around to the right to reach your starting point.

Walk 11

Little Bedwyn, Stype and Standen Manor

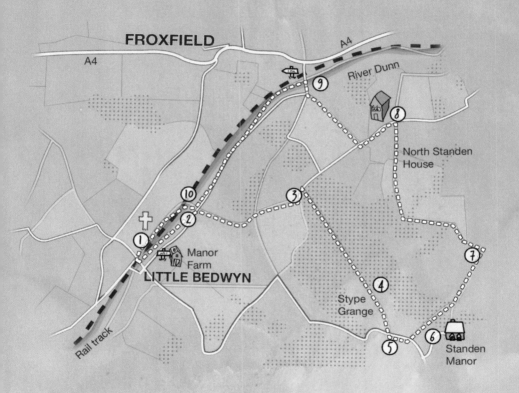

FROXFIELD

A4

A4

River Dunn

North Standen
House

Manor
Farm

LITTLE BEDWYN

Rail track

Stype
Grange

Standen
Manor

Walk 12

Little Bedwyn

Little Bedwyn is another lovely little village, situated on the Kennet and Avon canal, it has no pub, but does have an award winning restaurant called The Harrow. The walk is a longish one and may seem a little dull and hard work at first, but it's well worth persevering with and is quite varied. It's only a short detour to The Pelican and worth it as it's a nice pub with good food.

The Kennet and Avon Canal enjoyed its bicentenary in 2010. The once busy canal had fallen into a state of disrepair by the 1950s, but The Kennet and Avon Canal Trust, with the help of British Waterways and a £25 million lottery grant, restored the canal to the excellent state we see today.

Distance: 7 miles

Time: 2½ – 3 hours

OS map: Explorer 158

Time to **The Pelican pub**: 2 hours

1. Park near the church at **Little Bedwyn** (SU291662). Walk to end of road and turn right, following road out of village, and across crossroads.

2. Where road turns left continue on bridleway signed (faintly) '**To Harrow Farm**'. Follow the path between, then to the right of trees, then across open field until you reach minor road.

3. Turn right along road, briefly uphill, then downhill to the **A4**. Cross carefully and continue on minor road for a few metres, then take bridleway signposted '**Rudge**'.

4. Follow narrow bridleway for 800m then follow footpath arrow to left, up hill until you reach a minor road.

5. Turn left on road, then take marked footpath to the right after **Rudge Farmhouse**. Follow field edge keeping hedge to the right. Follow path left, then right through plantation to concrete track.

6. Turn left, then right, on track through coppice. Turn right at junction of tracks and footpath.

7. Continue on track, past tracks leading off on either side, and then turn right uphill on track opposite first of two footpaths to the left.

8. When track veers to the left continue on footpath with hedge then wood on left until you reach a minor road. Turn left for a few metres on road, then right on track towards **Cake Wood**, then take footpath to the right.

9. Follow footpath along edge of wood, then to the right between fields. Carry on to left of trees until you reach steps down to the **A4**. **The Pelican** is 100m to the right at this point.

10. Cross **A4** carefully and continue on opposite road over the railway and canal, then follow footpath sign on right to the **Kennet and Avon Canal**. Turn left and take canal towpath past three locks (and one bridge), then cross the canal at the next bridge, following footpath sign for Froxfield Road.

11. Cross railway line (with care), then turn immediately keeping the railway to your left. Cross a stile into an orchard, then continue past church and around to the right to reach your starting point.

Walk 12
Little Bedwyn

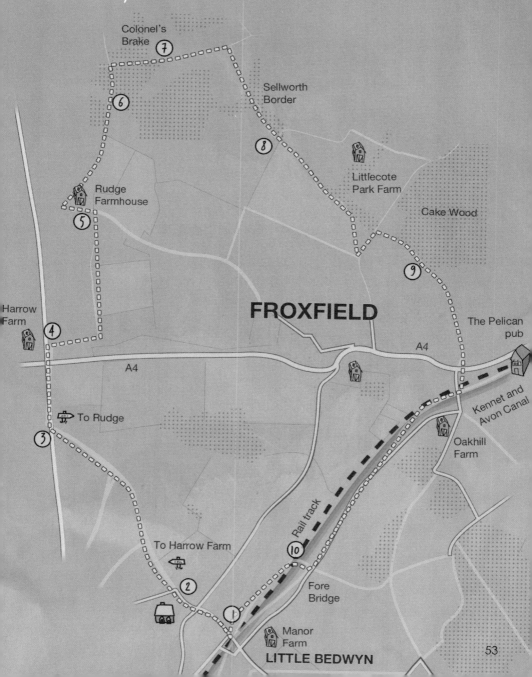

Colonel's Brake
⑦

Sellworth Border

⑥

⑧

Littlecote Park Farm

Cake Wood

Rudge Farmhouse
⑤

⑨

Harrow Farm
④

The Pelican pub

FROXFIELD

A4

A4

To Rudge

③

Kennet and Avon Canal

Oakhill Farm

Rail track

To Harrow Farm

⑩

②

Fore Bridge

①

Manor Farm

LITTLE BEDWYN

Walk 13

Aldbourne to Ramsbury

Ramsbury and Aldbourne are another two lovely villages just across the border into Wiltshire and have currently five pubs between them. This circular walk between the two is varied with some great views, it's quite hard work in places, with some steepish climbs. In late summer and autumn shorts are inadvisable as there is some long grass to wade through, and nettles to avoid.

Distance: 6½ miles

Time: 2¾ hours

OS map: Explorer 157

Time to **The Crown and Anchor** : 1½ hours

Time to **The Bell**: 1½ hours

1. Park next to the pond in **Aldbourne** (SU265757), opposite **The Crown pub**. Walk along the road towards Hungerford for about half a mile, past the mini roundabout and out of town, until you reach a gravel track on the left opposite a sign saying **Ford Farm Entrance**.

2. Take this track all the way to the top of the hill to a gate and stile with footpath signs. Cross the stile and proceed in a straight line across the field to reach a small gap in trees with yellow footpath sign.

3. Follow arrow through copse and out into corner of field and bear right, keeping to right edge of field right to the bottom corner where you will see a path.

4. Turn left onto the path and follow all the way up the hill, round two corners to the right, then at the end of the path turn left through a farmmetre and onto a lane. Turn right on lane.

5. Follow lane until it forks left and right. Bear slightly left and follow footpath sign (for **Ramsbury**) into field. The path is not clear so follow direction of sign across field to walk just to the right of the lone tree and to a stile leading into woods.

6. Cross this wobbly stile then carry straight on across alternative footpath to a kind of wooden frame (which used to be a stile) on the left. Duck through this and bear right along left edge of field.

7. Carry on all the way to bottom right edge of field. Cross stile and go through copse to next field and follow right edge of this field until you reach a path to a small footbridge, cross and follow path to road.

8. Cross road with care and cross stile. Bear slightly left then right to pass through farmyard, then skirt right round fence to take middle grassy path up the hill. Cross stile at top onto road and turn left, then immediately right onto path through trees.

9. Go through gate at end of path and go straight on, keeping the trees on your right, until you reach another gate. Go through kissing gate and carry on with the trees on your left this time, through another gate and down to road.

10. Turn right on road and walk for about 100m until the road curves left and there is a byway sign to **Swan's Bottom**. Follow this path. If you want to visit **Ramsbury** and either of its pubs stay on the road.

11. After another 100m turn sharp right on footpath between hedges. Follow this path up the hill and along the edge of a field. The path diverts briefly into copse, then out and back in again, follow until you reach a kissing gate.

More instructions overleaf »

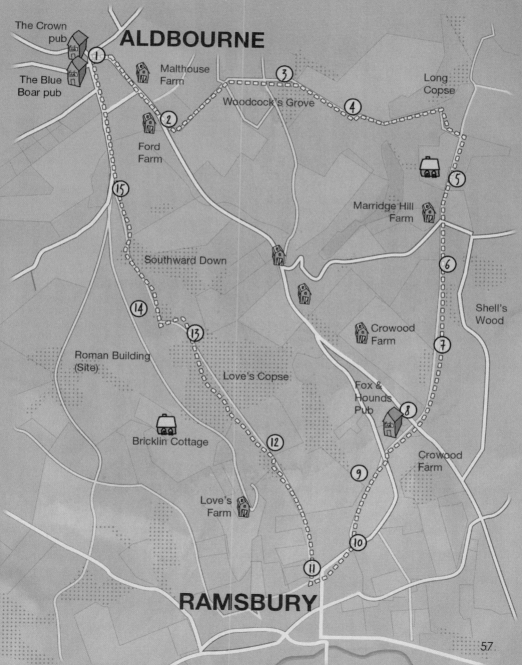

Walk 13
Aldbourne to Ramsbury

The Crown pub

ALDBOURNE

The Blue Boar pub

Malthouse Farm

Woodcock's Grove

Long Copse

Ford Farm

Marridge Hill Farm

Southward Down

Shell's Wood

Roman Building (Site)

Love's Copse

Crowood Farm

Fox & Hounds Pub

Bricklin Cottage

Love's Farm

Crowood Farm

RAMSBURY

12. Go diagonally left across field towards another gate and go through gate. Follow main path through **Love's Copse** (or if it's too muddy take the first left, then right and right again to get back to main path, and turn left). When you reach junction of paths continue straight on out of copse, then immediately right, back into copse and follow this path as it curls left and out of copse again.

13. Turn right and proceed with the hedgerow on your left until you see a yellow footpath sign on the left into copse, follow this path left until you near an exit on the left*. Exit and turn right, and right again to reach the far corner of the wood. *If the way is blocked with nettles turn right through wood and you can emerge near the far corner.

14. Follow path along left side of hedge (can be a bit overgrown) and continue as it bears left until you reach track. Follow track to the right of hedgerow, ignoring overgrown byway, and follow down to meet road.

15. Turn right on road down into **Aldbourne**. Where road turns right, go straight on into road called **The Butts**. Go right on larger road and at the end of this road cross the main road and bear right to **The Crown pub**, opposite the pond. (**The Blue Boar pub** is just up the small lane next to **The Crown**).

Walk 14

Aldbourne and the Downs

A tougher walk than many, with a long slow climb at the start, but the effort is rewarded with some nice views over the Downs. The Four Barrows that you pass fairly late on in the walk are thought to be Bronze Age burial mounds.

Distance: 6½ miles

Time: 2½ hours

OS map: Explorer 157

Time to **The Crown pub**: 2½ hours

Time to **The Blue Boar pub**: 2½ hours

1. Park by the pond in **Aldbourne** (SU265757), and walk up the small road to the right of **The Crown pub** towards the green. Pass **The Blue Boar pub** on your right and **Aldbourne Church** on your left and continue up the lane, keeping right when it forks.

2. Cross the road and continue on byway opposite until you reach another road. Cross this road carefully and take the byway opposite all the way up the long hill until you reach a road at the top.

3. Cross road carefully and at footpath sign opposite pass through gate and into field. The footpath should bear half left across field towards the **M4**, (but you may have to go left until you find the gap if the crops are high,) then turn left, walking next to the fence to reach the far corner of the field. Go up track to road and turn left.

4. Turn right at T-junction and walk along verge on right side of road for a few hundred metres until you see a bridle path sign on the left just after the fence starts to drop. Cross the road and take this path down to reach a gate on the left.

5. Pass through gate and follow the path downhill to reach a small road. Cross and take the byway opposite along left edge of field (the byway itself can be waterlogged, but you can walk just to the right of it). At corner follow path into copse and keep on path until you emerge from copse.

6. Follow the bridleway sign pointing left and follow path along left edge of field until you reach the **Four Barrows** (four small hillocks). Bear slightly left to reach gate, go through and continue on track opposite as it turns into a hedged path.

7. At end of track turn right on road and walk on the raised verge on the right. Pass through the churchmetre, then go down the steps and take the road opposite, along the right of the green, to emerge next to the pond.

Walk 14
Aldbourne and the Downs

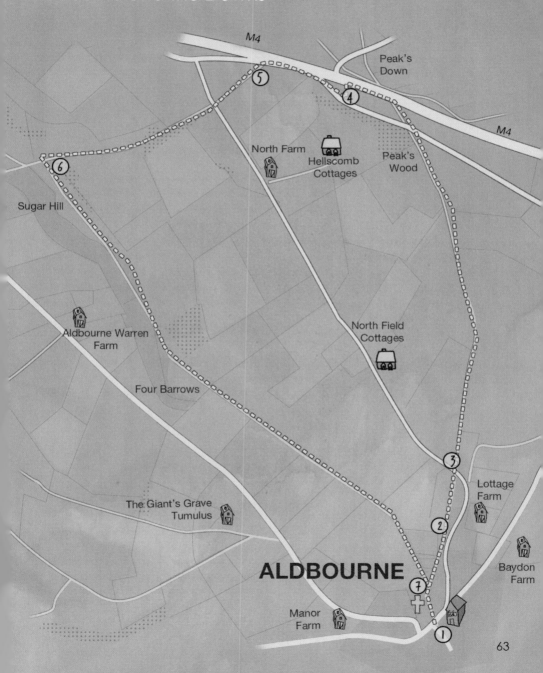

M4

Peak's Down

⑤

④

M4

North Farm

Hellscomb Cottages

Peak's Wood

Sugar Hill

⑥

Aldbourne Warren Farm

North Field Cottages

Four Barrows

The Giant's Grave Tumulus

③

Lottage Farm

②

Baydon Farm

ALDBOURNE

⑦

Manor Farm

①

The Bear Hotel at Hungerford

Enjoy the beauty of the North Wessex Downs
Fantastic Food, Local Ales, Great Atmosphere

Call us on 01488 682 512

or for more information visit our website:

www.thebearhotelhungerford.co.uk

The Bear Hotel
41 Charnham Street
Hungerford
Berkshire
RG17 0EL

THE HUNGERFORD BOOKSHOP

www.hungerfordbooks.co.uk

Tel: 01488 683480 email: sales@hungerfordbooks.co.uk

We are an award-winning independent bookshop, situated on the high street in the historical town of Hungerford. Do come in and visit us to see our full range of books, hand-picked with care. You will find the latest paperbacks, hot-off-the-press hardbacks, sumptuous coffee table books, and a good Children's section to feed hungry young minds! We also stock over 4,000 second hand and antiquarian books downstairs. We are always happy to advise, and are able to order in titles that will usually arrive the next day. We also hold regular author events – sign-up to our mailing list to be kept informed.

- Free fast ordering service
- Personalised service to find the right book
- Generous loyalty card scheme for adults and children
- Out of print ordering service (a small charge will apply)
- A basement of secondhand and antiquarian books
- DVDs
- Cards, giftwrap and notebooks
- Calendars and diaries
- Bookmarks, bookrests and reading lights
- Hungerford Bookshop Vouchers and National Gift Cards
- Regular author events (sign-up to our mailing list)

We are open from:
9.30 a.m. – 5 p.m. every Monday to Friday
9.30 a.m. – 5.30 p.m. on Saturdays
And some Sundays approaching Christmas – please ask

Follow us on Twitter @hungerfordbooks and join 'Friends of The Hungerford Bookshop' on Facebook
The Hungerford Bookshop, 24 High Street, Hungerford, Berkshire, RG17 0NF

About the author

Alex Milne-White has lived in Hungerford for five years and owns and runs The Hungerford Bookshop with his wife, Emma.